JESUS CHRIST
THE BEST KING OF ALL

JESUS CHRIST
THE BEST KING OF ALL

CATHERINE MACKENZIE

CF4•K

10 9 8 7 6 5 4 3 2 1
© Copyright 2010 Christian Focus Publications
ISBN 978-1-84550-568-4
Published in 2010 by
Christian Focus Publications,
Geanies House, Fearn, Tain,
Ross-shire, IV20 1TW,
Great Britain
Cover design by Daniel van Straaten
Illustrations by Fred Apps
Printed in China
Scripture taken from the Contemporary English Version © 1991, 1992,
1995 by American Bible Society, Used by Permission.

A child has been born for us.
We have been given a son who will be our ruler.
His names will be Wonderful Adviser and Mighty God,
Eternal Father and Prince of Peace.
Isaiah 9: 6

THE BABY AND
THE STABLE

If you were a king you'd live in a palace with a soft bed and wonderful clothes.

But Jesus is a different king, a better king. He is the best king of all.

Mary was an ordinary girl but a special one too. She wasn't from a rich family. However, God chose her to be the mother of the Son of God.

When an angel told her she was going to have a baby, Mary was surprised. 'I am not even married!' she gasped.

The angel told Mary that the power of God would come over her. When the baby was born she was to call him 'Jesus'.

Mary had promised to marry Joseph. So God sent an angel to tell him that this baby was God's Son. Joseph was happy to marry Mary then.

After the wedding the Romans decided to count all the people in Israel.

Everyone went to their home town to be counted. Joseph took Mary to Bethlehem.

When they arrived in Bethlehem it was very busy. They could not find a room to sleep in. Mary had to give birth to the baby Jesus in

a stable. Jesus was placed in a manger for a cot and wrapped in strips of cloth.

But the stable was not a palace! The manger was not a soft bed! Strips of cloth were not a king's clothes. Why did Jesus not have all these things that other kings have?

This is because Jesus is a different King. He is the most important King ever. Jesus died to save sinners.

Sin must be punished. But Jesus was punished even though he never sinned. He allowed this to happen so that his people could be saved from sin and the punishment they deserved.

In the Bible: read about the baby Jesus in Matthew chapter 2.

THE SHEPHERDS AND THE ANGELS

If you were a king you would be very important. Your soldiers would obey all your instructions.

But Jesus is a different king, a better king. He is the best king of all.

When Jesus was born people didn't know how special he really was. But some shepherds soon found out.

They were out in the fields one night when an angel of the Lord appeared.

Everything shone brightly. The shepherds were scared. The angel said, 'Don't be afraid. I have good and joyful news for you. Today,

in Bethlehem, a Saviour has been born, Christ the Lord. You will find the baby wrapped in strips of cloth and lying in a manger.'

Suddenly more angels appeared. They all sang praises to God! 'Glory to God in the Highest and on earth

peace to men on whom his favour rests.' The shepherds knew that this baby must be really special!

They ran to Bethlehem and found the baby Jesus in a manger just as the angel had said.

The shepherds told everyone about what they had seen. Everyone who heard their story was amazed!

Now shepherds aren't soldiers. They have sheep instead of swords. A king doesn't have an army of shepherds.

But Jesus is a different King. He was born to bring peace to earth. He will give you peace in your heart if you make him your King.

In the Bible: read about the shepherds and the baby Jesus in Luke chapter 2.

SIMEON, ANNA AND THE PROMISED SAVIOUR

If you were a king you would have feasts and servants to obey you.

But Jesus is a different king, a better king. He is the best king of all.

Very few people knew how special Jesus was when he was a baby but two people were delighted to see him.

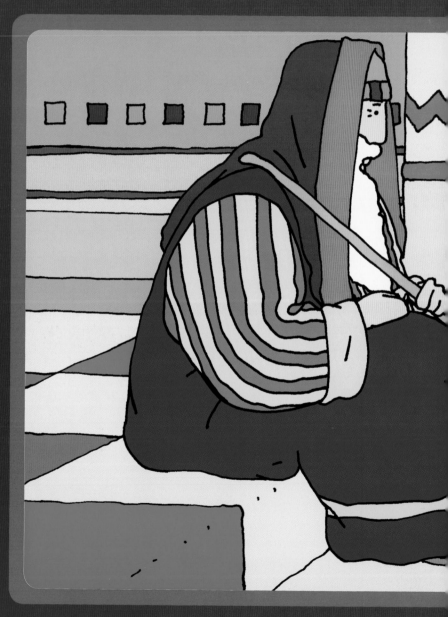

One old man called Simeon was at the temple waiting for God's special king. God had told him he would see him one day.

Mary and Joseph took the baby Jesus to the temple for the first time. Simeon knew he was God's promised Saviour who had come

to save those who trusted in God. Simeon reached out and held the baby Jesus in his arms.

'I can die in peace now,' he said. 'I have seen God's Saviour.'

Mary and Joseph were astonished.
What an amazing thing to say
about their baby! Simeon then

explained to Mary that her child
was very important but that she
would feel very sad sometimes.

'A sword will pierce your
own soul too,' Simeon told
her.

Just then an old lady called Anna arrived. She was always in the temple day and night praying to God.

She gave thanks when she saw the baby Jesus. Anna knew that God had sent Jesus to save his people.

Anna spoke about the child Jesus to all the people who were looking forward to God's promised Saviour.

But two old people aren't the crowds you'd expect when a king arrives. This is because Jesus is a different king. He came to die on

a cross and not to fight with a sword. If you trust in him he will give you a life that will never end.

In the Bible: read about Simeon and Anna in Luke chapter 2.

THE WISE MEN AND THEIR GIFTS

If you were a king you would wear a great crown. Other rulers would visit you and listen to everything you had to say.

But Jesus is a different king, a better king. He is the best king of all.

In the East some wise men saw a star. They knew that a special king had been born in Israel. The wise men travelled to Jerusalem to King Herod's palace.

'Where is the new king?' they asked. 'We want to worship him.'

Herod didn't know the answer to their question. He had to ask the priests and teachers of the law for the answer.

They told him that God's promised Saviour would be born in Bethlehem in Judea. Because that was what was written in God's Word.

Herod wasn't happy. He secretly asked the wise men some questions and then he gave them some instructions.

'Go and search carefully for the child. When you find him report to me so that I too may worship him.'

However, Herod was really plotting to kill the baby Jesus. He didn't want to worship him at all. The wise men did however, and after they had listened to Herod they

went on their way. The star that they had seen in the East went ahead of them. It stopped at the house where Jesus was.

The wise men worshipped him. Then an angel warned them that Herod planned to kill the child. The wise men decided to leave immediately.

They would not go back to King Herod and would return to their country by another route.

But before the wise men left they gave Jesus gifts of gold, frankincense and myrrh.

Costly gifts like these are often given to kings and rulers. But the gift that Jesus wants most is for you to love and trust in him.

In the Bible: read about the baby Jesus and the wise men in Matthew chapter 2.

CHRISTIAN FOCUS PUBLICATIONS

F H •K M

Christian   Christian   CF4K   Mentor
Focus   Heritage

Christian Focus Publications publishes books for adults and children under its four main imprints: Christian Focus, Christian Heritage, CF4K and Mentor. Our books reflect that God's word is reliable and Jesus is the way to know him, and live for ever with him.

Our children's publication list includes a Sunday school curriculum that covers pre-school to early teens; puzzle and activity books. We also publish personal and family devotional titles, biographies and inspirational stories that children will love.

If you are looking for quality Bible teaching for children then we have an excellent range of Bible story and age specific theological books. From pre-school to teenage fiction, we have it covered!

**Find us at our web page:
www.christianfocus.com**

CF4•K
Because you're never
too young to know Jesus